# The Corporate
# Escape Plan

## A Practical Guide to
## Professional Freedom

J.S.Vermeer

I0484914

Jigsaw Piece Publishing

London, England

Providence has nothing good or high in store for one who does not resolutely aim at something high or good. A purpose is the eternal condition of success.

T. T. Munger

# 1. An invitation

**This is not a whimsical self help book.** It is a practical guide and plan to leaving a large corporation and setting up an independent business. It tackles this task by getting at the root issue as to why so many of us settle for a comparatively unfulfilling life in large faceless and often ethically conflicted organisations. This guide goes on to advise on reconstructing our approach to purpose, professional value and how to develop these qualities in a meaningful way that is capable of generating sustainable streams of income. There are many methods and tools that are freely available to anyone in the pursuit of professional independence who have become disenfranchised with the large company promise of happiness. This guide advocates a series of steps to prepare for the first solo flight many of which many can be prepared and undertaken whilst still in the bosom of corporate employment.

The author of the book spent 15 years working for global companies in mid and senior management positions. He then left to work as a consultant and followed the process highlighted in these pages. He now consults into the board level of large public and private corporations, changing their technologies and processes to operate effectively in the digital age where information is king. He chooses the jobs he takes on (mostly the exciting ones that create positive changes for people and the business). He generally selects where and how he works; he employs associates on an as needed basis; he makes considerably more than he did working for a large corporation; and with the freedom with which his small but potent company executes, he is considerably happier. He invites you to join his lifestyle.

Big changes are started by the few. They always have been and this will continue to be the case.

# 2. The nature of the relationship with your company

Congratulations, you have gotten this far. I'm serious. You are are stealing some time to reflect on your position. You are probably reading this on some form of public transport or in bed. How do I know this? Because I am you. Together we constitute 70% of the working population. Approaching mid-life, a mortgage, wife, young kids, decent holiday twice a year, moved to the suburbs, a few hobbies and romance when the atmospheric conditions prevail. Generally a loving and wholesome life geared mostly, and through choice, towards others. However 99% of my time is either working or with the family so to find a moment to reflect is rare. So when I say congratulations, I mean it!

Until two years ago, I had spent my life as a salary man. Forging a career in blue chip organisations in technology divisions either sourcing or developing technology services across the globe. However, gradually over a 15 year career, I became increasingly trapped. My degrees of freedom had rapidly diminished and constraints in my life had increased. My salary had improved quite significantly, however my personal well being had not. Don't get me wrong - the satisfaction from having a family was and still is amazing, but the levels of actualising and being in charge of my own professional destiny had taken a nose dive.

Some may say *it's just a job*, a means to an end; you work to live and the rest of the bullshit rhetoric. It isn't just a job. Its something that you spend a great deal of your time doing and as such, to some degree, it defines you. Maybe not to others outside of work, but it defines you to yourself and to a large extent to others in the social arena of the workplace. Most people spend 75 - 85% of their waking year doing their job or travelling to and from their place of work. It's an enormous commitment that affects many levels of the human psyche.

Naturally, any of us could walk out the office door and not return, but corporate entrapment is not as simple as that. It is multi-faceted and complex to deconstruct. I use the word entrapment or "trap" in a non malicious way as for the most it is self-imposed and a psychological phenomenon. To use a dictionary definition of a trap: *"A device to retain animals, allowing entry but not exit"*.

I think it is equally important at this stage to share an understanding of the opposite of corporate entrapment. Namely, professional freedom, as this is the ultimate objective of this book.

To provide the reader - "you" - with an escape plan. Professional freedom can be described as: "The freedom of choice in how to spend time delivering value to others and through this act generating surpluses (profits) for oneself."

So let's turn the clock back and try to understand why we are how we are. Our parents, for most, were born during or not long after the last World War. Using Abraham Maslow's "Hierarchy of Needs (A Theory of Human Motivation)" as a baseline, these guys were at the bottom of Maslow's scale of motivators in life. Their world and existence had been fundamentally threatened and consequently they were in search of security. Complete socio-economic security. Security that their houses would not be bombed, security that toilet roll would be available in shops, and the security of a predictable income stream that had the potential to grow and give them stability to bring up a family. Now enters the large corporation and its paternalistic promise. Society at this point was being run as a command society, where the country's survival, and therefore your parent's survival, depended a lot upon the actions of the central state. Therefore the command and control of the "paternal" organisation simply followed the social programming prevailing at the time.

The company was generally considered as the "good company" that created certainty, was dependable and that shaped and nurtured its social asset "staff". There were trade unions that supported the rights of the employee when the board got to overly demanding, clear career plans for the individual and modest growth expectations for the business. Hours of work provided for a work life balance and everyone lived in harmony. Our parents were brought up and educated to join this salvation by the corporate world and likewise many of them, with the help of the education system, passed these values and beliefs onto us. A set of values that steer the individual from a very young age to join an established set of disciplines that will lead to acceptance in the corporate world. A value system that emphasises the need for us to belong, to be taken care of, to follow rules and guidelines, to learn facts, and adapt to established processes. A value system designed to defer our autonomy and personal freedom to a greater "unknown good" and to allow for minimal creative ownership over our thoughts and lives.

So what changed? Answer: A whole lot.

Firstly, the social context of the organisation changed. As the global financial system developed, the organisation transcended national boundaries. Their national construct disappeared and with it any sense of sovereign identity. Secondly, the trade unions were dissolved, leaving the employee largely defenceless while the judiciary system was (and still is) designed to err on the side of those with the most money, namely large companies. Thirdly, technology and communication became expansive leading to information transparency and the growth of the information economy.

Silently, and concurrently in the background, there has been the slow deterioration in the central power of the state. A deterioration that has now arrived at its final chapter through the invention of the internet, and true democratisation through the use of communication tools such as social media and crowd sourcing.

Arguably, this is what the internet was invented for after it grew out of ArpaNet in the 70's; a way to democratise society through the liberation of information, social assets, and communication. A means for societies to connect and self organise so that the relevance of a paternalistic culture become less and less over time.

With a structured social network capable or creating and sharing services, support, and value the need for large hierarchical public and private organisations has gone into decline. In fact, it is my prediction that in the next 20 years power hierarchies will only remain where there is a natural monopoly such as oil and gas or water or Google. For the rest, organisations will flatten and eventually disband, first into nodal professional communities and then into loose alliances of the like minded. Power structures will become unpopular and dismantled.

The result of all this has been a clear separation of large corporations from societal values: Your values. The employment contract has become a voluntary agreement, not a pledge or a commitment. It is now a temporary vehicle for aligning mutual interest. Most of its clauses are designed for ease of separation rather than collaboration and mutual growth.

So where does this leave you? Well, it left me after the better part of a decade stuck in a "Global Head" role working for a global financial services company doing a 12 hour shift managing a team across the 3 regional time zones. The organisation was forever consolidating and every month or so someone new was vaporised from their seat and summarily replaced with a contractor. The company amongst the many truly global companies had good heritage and a strong culture but, just like many others of its ilk, it had slowly but surely succumb to the global capitalist squeeze. Senior management had been axed and career progression was futile as more middle managers competed for fewer positions. Further to this, my role was relatively specialised and I was relatively good at it. So upper management wanted me to remain in situ. No change required. So, every year, I was given the classic "opiate" performance review. I call it the "opiate review" as it acknowledged that you had done a good job, invented some bullshit area that you could still develop, delivered a bonus sufficient to stop you complaining and yet failed to acknowledge a case for immediate change. It was just enough to keep you off the job sites for a few months.

Many of my contemporaries at the time were just waiting for the pay off. Braving up to the next redundancy round with all the mixed feelings that a sudden injection of capital and immediate ostracisation can render. Does any of this sound familiar? However, what I noticed about the many in waiting for their golden parachute was their level of general unhappiness with their lives. Or at least with their working lives. Their passion for their discipline had dried up and consequently they irradiated a type of mediocrity that can only be associated with someone who is begrudgingly tolerating a lifestyle. They were not the few; they were by far the majority. A whole building full of people no longer at the helm of their lives, instead being towed along by a corporate machine at the whim of a spreadsheet in the hands of somebody they have not met before or pretend to understand.

Moreover, the more I began to recognise the "impassives" in the company, the more I realised I was fast becoming one of them. My professional life had become a tolerable discomfort. How long had it been that way? No idea - perhaps two maybe three years. Maybe I had just clung on through the birth of my two sons; maybe the recession, maybe any number of reasons. Who knows. However, what quickly dawned on me was that I was not an Impassive. Or at least I desperately didn't want to be one. I had not studied, travelled, and worked like a brute over the years to end up as a faceless suit tethered to the middle ranks of a global bureaucracy hoping and waiting for someone to make me surplus to requirements. That didn't form part of my childhood life ambition and 38 years later it still didn't.

So I resolved to become someone who I wanted to be. To forget compromises and excuses and to escape the arid and sterile corporate rut I had found myself in.

**Design Principle 1:** Do not wait around for the pay off unless it is imminent and certain. Your time is of greater value.

# 3. Getting over active inertia

Active inertia is an idea closely identified with Donald Sull, an associate professor at London Business School. It loosely defines the human state of the professional rut. Namely where the professional gets so programmed by routine, corporate values, and lack of creative stimuli that there is no appetite or will to engineer change. However, I would like to add that there can be a situation where there is an appetite to engineer change but the switching costs are considered too high or risk too great or both. Or potentially the gap between current state and desired state is perceived as too large. For the ardent Impassive, there is also the element of effort. Routine may lead to a psychological destruction of will and low self esteem but it generally get's easier over time. To change routine will require effort and discipline and a "can be bothered" attitude.

It was slightly ironic that my role in the global financial services company was focused on outsourcing and transformation; however I had become the professional sum of all the routines I performed. So on reflection I can see there are a few stages in getting past active inertia. They are as follows:

1. **Self assessment and diagnosis**
2. **Establish unique value**
3. **Setting up the shop front**
4. **The half way house**
5. **All systems go**

# 4. Self assessment

Self diagnosis is the single most important part of the Corporate Escape Plan. And, as you are this far through the book, undoubtedly you have started to explore whether you have escape potential as apposed to being a resident Impassive or alternatively a well satisfied and engaged employee. Incidentally, if you are the latter then I take my hat off to you. I have no criticism of those that have found contentment and reward within the corporate edifice. If you're on to a good thing, you are amongst the lucky few and this book is not for you.

This book targets the pioneer as I suggest those pioneering change outside of the corporate fortress have as just as many challenges to overcome as many of the explorers, past and present, who have taken forward steps through belief in themselves and conviction in purpose.

Self diagnosis is not easy and can take a lot of pride swallowing. Firstly, understand your value in the context of your organisation. It is essential to understand that if you have survived the countless number of restructuring activities your company has undertaken, if you continue to get good performance reviews, and if you are punctual and execute well and with respect for your staff, peers, and management, then I think it is fair to say that you're of significant value to your organisation. The issue at hand is that the organisation has become significantly less valuable to you. The financial package and the experience of work are no longer of interest or at least have become comparably less interesting.

I, like the droves of disinterested people across my company floor, had my head down in my shared space focusing with all my might on producing the next piece of analysis, strategy, or delivery plan. It was then that I realised that my fixation and focus was not to produce accuracy or quality but to stop myself considering an alternative way of spending my time. This was an important realisation. To quote one of the most challenged people in our recent history, Helen Keller: "Science may have found a cure for most evils; but it has found no remedy for the worst of them all - the apathy of human beings."

In my case, I woke up more or less the moment I self diagnosed. My professional identity was not good enough. I was intrinsically unhappy with the level I was operating at. I was not being brave, I was not actualising, and I was not becoming somebody that I wanted to be. I had recognised that my children would neither admire me nor learn from me if I continued to lean on them as pretexts for safety and lack of professional accomplishment.

So to summarise the tick boxes for self diagnosis, they are as follows:

1. You find yourself looking around you're work area and fail to comprehend why your colleagues who complain daily about their routines are still doing them.
2. You are no longer interested in describing what you do to a member of the family or friend.
3. You have come up with at least 3 radical ideas in the last 12 months regarding how to improve your professional life, though not one has been implemented.
4. You would rather paint a white wall with white paint than do your daily set of tasks.

If two or more of the above apply to your professional sentiment over the majority of your working days, you are suffering from Active Inertia. NOTE, THIS IS NOT A REASON TO BE GLUM. Acknowledging this is a MAJOR breakthrough and arguably a clear diagnosis of the malady is a very good result. It means it's time for change - if you are willing.

**Escape Principle 2:** Diagnosis of Active Inertia is a good thing and means that change can begin.

# 5. Pioneering unique value

A frontiersman or explorer: "Pioneer". Distinctive and individual: "Unique". The usefulness of something: "Value". Unique, useful and ahead of the game.

Right, so you have a graduate degree, you may have a masters or PHD, you've done your internal training courses on management, leadership, process design, working in teams. You've been in a semi-skilled function for 5 or 10 years. Let's face it most jobs in the white collar market place can be relatively easily learnt. Most tasks could be taught to the average 16 year old. It is the organisational context and the experience to deal with specific situations or projects that keep you in a role. AND, by the way, this is precisely where the organisation wants to keep you. Specific to your job and specific to the company. Not unique enough to easily command an external demand and not generic enough so as to not add discernible value to operations. That's where they want you, right there, right there bang in the middle. Dispensable yet relevant to task.

Why dispensable yet relevant to task? Well you know why. It's to manage your perception of your value, to reduce the flight risk of good performers. Whether explicitly or implicitly communicated, this is a key mechanism for a company to retain its staff. If you are over confident you can become disruptive and/or a threat to management. As a general rule humility accompanied by intervals of self deprecation will keep you in good train as long as your delivery is strong.

ALL of this is of course a gross generalisation. There are good managers that can lead and there are also effective managers who can restrain and control. Although the latter will only retain staff throughout a recession. The majority of employees want to be affiliated with someone who is leading and creating charge. This creates a cause and a cause is more fulfilling than being controlled and restrained.

So, in an ideal world the corporate and the individual interests sufficiently overlap to create harmony, reduce personnel churn, redundancy, and litigation; the corporate world is a sweet happy place and employees skip to work in a Dickensian fashion . Very unlikely!

So how do we create value in ourselves that will make our services purchasable on the open market?

The pioneering of unique value works on various levels.   It serves to stimulate the creative mind, the right side of the mind that has been pounded into submission by routine time and time again. This in itself generates a good feeling. We are born to create and develop and learn. It is part of the human condition. To stop this process early on in adulthood is inhumane and over times extinguishes our spirit.

Unique value serves to differentiate us. Consultants love flowery terms such as your "personal brand" and describe you as a product or service. This is all analogous flim-flam used to describe specialisation. Frederick Taylor in his research on scientific management realised well over 100 years ago that specialisation creates value. Over the next 10 years from now, the hierarchical organisation will collapse and personal specialisation will bloom. Companies will become loose coalitions of like-minded mixed specialists operating as a fluid whole capable of adapting and changing rapidly to new sources of information.

Unique value also feeds our ambition and our self esteem. To state the obvious, to be a specialist at something is to be professionally special. To hold a unique set of qualities. To be part of a restricted supply and therefore to hold a greater value, assuming a decent level of demand.

Personal demand, individual value, professional specialism - aren't those great words? Don't they lift you out of your cube or shared desk space? Okay, so you have a degree in history and an MBA and you've been a Project Manager for 7 years in the IT department of a global company. If this floats your boat then fair enough further develop these skills, update your Prince 2 course, study ITIL and other such institutional semi-skilled courses. Alternatively, if this is humdrum to you, shake it up. Find something more appealing, more special. However, find something that builds upon rather than negates your experience. An example may be "the programme management of emergency and disaster support services" or "the psychology of managing large transformation programmes in dysfunctional public institutions". Take your profession and value and develop it somewhere else. I think it was Steve Jobs who said that: "Creativity is not the development of something new; it is the combining of existing ideas and principles to form a unique proposition." And if he didn't say it - then he most certainly should have.

If you get stuck or find that the last years have filled your life with a large amount of the unspecific and the uninteresting, then I recommend that you take the following approaches to reassessing purpose and discovering your specific interest:

First, look back to your prepubescent years, before your professional life started and your personal life began to get more complicated, and try and recall your ambition or hobby. What was it that you did voluntarily that made you feel good about yourself? Reflect on this for some time. There were activities that you were "encouraged' to do, however normally there are one or two that you would have sacrificed watching television for or at least that became your second choice after the goggle box was turned off.

Second, look forward to your future self and try to envisage the challenges that will be increasingly encountered in future society and what skills and competencies you may be able to develop to assist others in these challenges. Consultants call this process "horizon scanning". I conducted both these exercises and realised that I had two specific interests. The first was "recovery and restoration" - as a child I worked with injured animals in animal protection shelters, but I also spent a lot of time in restoring generally anything that could be restored (e.g. bikes, toys etc.). The second area that always fascinated me was technology, in particular how it enabled communication. My parents were separated by culture, divorce, and continents and I was reliant on technology to stay in touch with one half of my family. Some years later the internet was spawned by the same human need to inter-connect or inter-network.

Therefore, it is by no coincidence that I chose to specialise in *leading the transformation of health services to become more effective through advances in information and communications technology, and more specifically, web based services.*

Introspection and reconciling your findings regarding early life interests with future trends may take a while, although it can be a very exciting and revealing process. Much of how we develop is firmly embedded in the subconscious, so for the majority of the time your desired professional discipline will be in someway affiliated to your early life goals and where you see the future taking you. What is essential is that when you establish the description of your specific interest that: a) You write it out as a mission statement of unique value, and b) You stick to its core purpose. The core purpose should clearly state what you want to achieve and how you want to achieve it. By cementing the core purpose, you can start to build your Knowledge Base.

Constructing the Knowledge Base

The Knowledge Base is to preserve time by boxing clever. Time is our scarcest resource and has the greatest impact on ourselves, and thereafter others. We must use it shrewdly and to the greatest value. As I write, I am in a Spanish fishing village, in a rental villa, on a couch, in my underwear, overlooking the Mediterranean at 6:30 in the morning. Why? Because everybody is fast asleep upstairs, I'm listening to Ben Howard, the sun is rising, the coffee is working, and I have the space to think and write. Rare, selfish, and beautiful moments.

So, how do we improve the efficiency of gathering information? Well, obviously, we have the internet, so I won't propose egg sucking. However, there are now free lessons on the internet given by very reputable lecturers. Check "coursera.com" or "linda.com". I have followed courses from both of these online educational facilities. A list of tools and resources can be found in the penultimate section of this guide. The goal here is not to become just a specialist in your chosen field; it is to become "the specialist". There is an important distinction here and it doesn't happen overnight. This is why this guide focuses on building upon your existing foundation of experience rather than a complete reinvention of the professional self. The latter is possible but achieving "the specialist" status then becomes exponentially more challenging - not impossible, just a steeper hill rather than a gradual incline.

The Knowledge Base is an "easily accessible store of information and experience that can be used to increase unique value through specialist insight". Below are some recommended approaches in building this foundation layer for your specialism.

1. Using your existing company resources. This is a useful, if not slightly precarious, platform for development. If you are

perceived by your company as a flight risk, they will soon pick up on it. That is unless there is a short-term practical application for the study. In all situations, do not make a commitment to the company that you will only later have to buy your way out of. This only complicates severance and increases the psychological and financial switching costs. So, not good. However, if they are offering free internal courses on project management or financial analysis or, for that matter, anything that can serve the dual purposes of helping your existing job and supporting your specialist development, then make hay while the sun shines. However, steer away from anything that may create future conflict with your organisation. Your existing organisation is a social network and sitting sales opportunity that you want to keep in tact.

2. Using your network. Whether you use it actively or not - whether you are a natural networker or not - your existing company and its related organisations presents a wealth of social opportunity. Opportunism must be embraced as a good thing when developing unique value. The word "opportunism" for some reason carries negative connotations, although where there exists mutual benefit there can be nothing negative about it. Mutual benefit is the cornerstone of all life as we know it. So don't be bashful or get caught up in ethics. Use your network. Search out who in the company is operating in your future space either professionally or just as a general interest, and take them for a coffee. Search again, and repeat. It's easy, it's fun, and you will learn a lot about the possibilities and limitations in the sector and/or special-

ism. Also do not fear wasting people's time. They will appreciate the networking opportunity and showing interest in someone professionally is invariably received well.

3. Investment in your equity. Alright, so this step requires a little resource (other than time) but it is minimal, or at least it can be. First, I would recommend the purchase of a decent notebook. I personally use an Apple Macbook Air. They are light, portable, and reasonably powerful. However, they do not have a built in wifi and have some compatibility issues with mainstream business applications which are still very Windows orientated. If required, you can use Parallels, which is a downloadable service that creates a Windows Operating System on the Mac. Alternatively, use any suitably sturdy piece of hardware that is presentable, durable, and reflects well on the quality of your specialist organisation. Namely, you. Having this asset will allow you to work while on the move and in the spaces you can find in your working day. It will allow you to start to research and compile your professional library. Whether it's is a document library, a web favourites library, a video, an ebook, or podcast library ensure that a) you categorise well and b) make it easy to access and search. Information only has value when it is accessible.

4. Shadow a specialist. This does not mean stalking a stranger, but with a friend's of a colleague's consent. You may want to spend a few days working with them, accompanying them to client meetings, and potentially assisting them with prepara-

tion. This will provide a good indication for what resources they use and how they allocate their time.

5. Re-train. Finally, paid retraining may be required for the step change. However, which course and how it is attended is a much broader subject area and outside of the scope of this guide, which focuses on independent initiatives.

**Escape Principle 3.** Connect to a unique and genuine interest that will assist others.

**Escape Principle 4.** Build the Knowledge Base, tailored and easily accessible.

# 6. Shop front set up

The shop front is your calling card, a testament to your credibility. It's also a very cathartic and creative set of activities. Although here we just discuss set up, the reality is that, just like any shop front, your shop will require ongoing updates, maintenance, and change. Naturally, here we are using the shop front as a metaphor for any form of simple and lasting marketing activity that will clearly communicate your unique value proposition or tradable product or service. I will stick with the term "value proposition" for the purposes of this guide as it covers all bases and seems to have become a relatively well-known term.

Okay, so to get through the humdrum, here are a few basic considerations. Firstly, you are doing this to create revenue and surplus and not as a hobby, so we are looking to maximise business potential and professional satisfaction. Secondly, at this stage I expect that most of you are still working for a corporation, and therefore should not compromise your employment contract. We need to keep the company sweet, remember! Thirdly, the set up should be simple, low cost, low maintenance, and easy to communicate.

If we turned the clock back 16 years, the set up was largely a paper driven exercise, namely: print advertising, business cards, letter headed paper, incorporation, combined with a degree of public relations, trade shows and networking activities. Today, most of the above can be achieved online and with comparatively minimal effort. So what follows is a basic recipe for setting up a shop front. Again, this can be tailored to your value proposition and business plan.

1.  The elevator pitch. Cliché, I agree but more necessary now than ever before. As prophesied earlier in this book, as large companies fragment, the number of small organisations and independent traders will grow geometrically. Therefore, whatever it is that you will specialise in you will need to be able to say it between floors in an elevator clearly and succinctly. My elevator pitch, for example, is: "I use new information and communications technology to transform and improve healthcare operations." Another example may be: "I develop behavioural models for financial traders to alert management of risk taking." The key here is: "what you do" and "for whom". Implicit in the statement should be the "why". The person then leaves the exchange understanding how your operation applies to them or somebody they know. Naturally, in reality these statements are used to open discussion and introduce ourselves. However, the chances are that if you can not articulate your elevator pitch well and explain why it meets a problem in the market, you will have trouble selling your services. Without exception, every

entrepreneur that I have met that has been unable to articulate their business proposition has been forced to undertake a re-modeling of their business. I once met a genius who explained to me at length her business' goal of "connecting the communication fabric behind multiple points of social networking in order to reengineer the conversation between government and the public." To this day I still have no idea what she does - and I'm a technologist!

2. Branding around the elevator pitch. One can have more than one elevator pitch or potentially multiple propositions nested within one pitch. Whatever the approach, follow the golden rule: KEEP IT SIMPLE. Personally, I intensely dislike the word "brand" - it evokes images of Pepsi and burnt cow hide. However, in the context of this book, a brand is nothing more than a recognisable message. Your brand can simply be your name. In the world of celebrity and politician (a rapidly converging set of occupations), your name is often your brand. In business, it is often perceived as the company name, logo, and key proposition(s) accompanied by some general graphical representations in print or online. However, in reality, a brand is a lot more than this. It is everything that you are discernibly connected or associated with. For example, for convenience I visited a local Italian restaurant, of the non-Italian variety and asked if they did a takeaway pizza as the kids were tired and destined to ruin someone's evening out had we ventured to a real restaurant. They had pizza boxes and

were good to go. On the wall, I noticed some captivating works of original art. Deeply textured abstracts with vivid colours. Each selling between £1,500 and £7,000. I studied the clientele seated in the restaurant and asked the waitress if the painter had sold any of his work. She replied that in the three years they had been on the wall only one had sold. The owner of the restaurant had bought it. Out of sympathy, I imagine. The same is in the world of sole professional or small organisation. Make sure you are connected into the right "ecosystem" - another 25 cent word, but you understand what I mean. Your association with other professionals and organisations should support and enhance your brand. This includes: Their propositions, values, notoriety, extra-curricula activities, etc. Select carefully, as they will be referring, referencing, and in some cases representing you.

3. Okay, so here we have slipped from brand into social network. The social network phenomenon of our time is much written about, so I don't want to re-discover it in the pages of this guide. It is there, you need to use it, and it is a double edged sword. Like any tool, if you use it incorrectly you can damage rather than create value. linkedin.com is the default professional relational social network. However, there are many others that are specifically targeted at creating a market place. One such organisation is elance.com, although Elance is much more transactional and offshore crowd-sourcing centred. I will expand on these resources in the penultimate

section of this guide. For the time being follow a couple of general rules regarding your social network:

- In reference to 2 (above), be selective in choosing your connections. If you are receiving poor commentaries or responses from someone in the public space, act promptly.

- Be consistent with your value proposition, brand, and experience across all forms of media. One deviation will create suspicion and, from this, a lack of trust. Trust is probably the single most important generator of business outside of the core proposition. In most (if not all) businesses, trust in quality comes before price as an evaluation criteria.

- Reference your most notable work or interests. Do not reference individuals in your network without their consent.

- Ensure any social network activity while you are in the "Set Up" phase does not conflict with your employment contract or indicate imminent departure. This is likely to throw lighter fuel on the corporate bridges that you will be needing in the future.

- If you are going to use the network as a forum for posting or referencing content, then make sure it is current, relevant, and kept up to date. Old content or commentaries reflect badly on the specialists as specialists are either leading edge or dinosaurs. Rarely anything in between.

Lastly and this is the most stupidly simple piece of advice, although probably the most important: Keep your format clean and clear and eliminate any and all spelling mistakes. Lack of attention to detail is a road to nowhere. Simplicity reduces the required attention and room for error.

4. Web-presence. I left this last intentionally. It so easy to throw up a website these days but extremely difficult to set up a web presence that works as you need it to. We will cover the various options in more detail in Chapter 8. However, here are a few general rules for your website:

- Design: For a contemporary feel, the design should use a lot of white space, be two or maximum three tone, very few/no borders, no 3D buttons or bevels, no flash technology, and all the key messaging on the landing page and in view without scrolling. Any further detail on the propositions should be one click away. The same is applicable for client testimonials or other key content. Ensure your contact details are visible on the first page as well as the contact page.

- Provider: If you are using a website provider, choose a provider operating HTML5. The templates will be more extensible, mobile compatible, and have a more professional look and finish. I use WIX.com. However, ensure that if you require email, domain name registration, storage, search engine optimisation, or an e-commerce platform that you research the add-on costs before committing to any one component.


- Build: If you are having a website built for you by a web developer then, depending on its complexity, I would off-shore. elance.com, mentioned previously, is an easy and safe way to offshore web-site development. Completion is milestone driven and payment is put into escrow until the purchaser (you) are happy with the final product. A key tip here is to make sure that the person(s) that you choose to do the build are actually doing it and not subbing it out to an unknown third party.

Lastly, and to continue the point, a website is only as valuable as its accessibility. So if it's not easily findable, navigable, and linked to your social network, then it becomes largely a redundant article. The penultimate chapter of this book will help get your professional profile the exposure it truly deserves.

**Escape Principle 5:** Get the messaging of your service's value proposition(s) honed and polished before it is exposed to your public.

# 7. The half way house

Unlike a proverbial approach to a swimming pool, I recommend prudence in building the market for your services. The deep end will generally not force you to swim unless, and this is a major caveat, your "warm client network" is firmly in place and leering at you with open purses like children in a candy shop. If this is the case and you do have receptive client network, I would fully recommend a quick and painless corporate exit in pursuit of professional freedom. However, for the majority, this will not be the case, and you will not want to bet the house and children's schooling on an unknown and untested proposition. This is where the Half Way House option will support your corporate escape plan.

If your role in the corporation is external facing and the contacts that you face off to are your potential future customers, then the Half Way House is a relatively easy step forward and may not be necessary. If your role is internal facing, then I strongly suggest an initial move to a Half Way House. The overriding objective of the move is to join an organisation or group that delivers all the opportunity to develop your specialised business (unique value) without   excessive risk. Think of it as an "incubator" for your value proposition, giving you the security you need while you develop and test your ideas on the wider public, third parties, and internal stakeholders.

**The four key areas for Half Way House development include:**
- Honing of the value proposition(s) and elevator pitch
- Expanding and qualifying the warm customer base
- Creation of thought leadership and soap box rights
- Operating the sale

There are many alternative approaches on offer here that range from low to high risk. The lowest risk option would be to transfer within your company to a programme team, new acquisition, country launch, or emergent business unit where you can practice your specialism. However, "cake and eat it too" options are rare and still have you floating around on the corporate umbilical, which will inhibit independent market exposure and therefore professional development. The second least risky alternative is to moonlight outside of your contracted hours. Again, I recommend that you check your contract and clear this with your HR department. The part-time approach may allow you to loosely assess demand, but it can also easily backfire. Corporate hours are long, especially if you are commuting, and we all need rest to be able to focus and apply ourselves. The part-time approach is a bit like fantasy football:

It's overly superficial and, as a result, rarely takes off and can quickly demotivate or dissuade you from progressing. The medium risky option (and the option I would recommend), is to join a small to mid-size niche firm or consultancy that operates or has functions that operate in your specialist area. Ideally your role within the company will have business development objectives associated with it so as to be an effective platform for development.

When joining the niche firm, check your employment contract carefully. Find out what ownership rights the company has over the intellectual property that you produce. And what the restrictions are on approaching the customer base when you leave the organisation. Companies will have varying standards for these types of non-competitive or "weener clauses".

I initially moved to a consultancy that laid claim to everything and anything I produced. In theory any idea or creative plan I had they had a preemptive right to the associated Intellectual Property. Such clauses are difficult to enforce however they do inhibit independent creative thought so I would recommend either negotiating away the clause or looking at alternatives. The golden rule here is one of equity and ethics. Namely, do not use work time or tools exclusively for private gain, and do not act against your company's interest with clients while the company pays your salary. This latter point is a matter of integrity and clients will not appreciate being involved in unethical behaviour. Remember that you are responsible for your brand and you need to keep it firmly intact.

I recall that I was very open when interviewing for a

consultancy role. The partner asked where I would like to be in the company within 3 - 5 years and I replied that, with all due respect, my preference would be to not be in the consultancy. I knew the partner so the frankness was appreciated. What I would bring to his practice would be a proposition for health services technology infrastructure outsourcing, a sales pipeline and client revenue, while the company would give me the incubation period and reduced risk environment to get exposure to the market. After what amounted to a 2.5 year period of mutual gain, all bets were off, and so was I.

**Honing the value proposition and elevator pitch**

Clients are a high risk testing ground for freshly squeezed value propositions. You may have one or two chances, at best, depending on your familiarity with the client. With a new client contact, I would say one chance. Therefore, the value proposition needs to be refined, clear, and easily cost justified. By far, the best place to test your proposition is with work colleagues and friends.

Depending on the service or product, the proposition should:
- Address a problem or unmet demand that is specific to the client
- Have benefits expressed in the quantitative and qualitative value
- Follow a deductive and logical argument
- Clearly differentiate itself from market alternatives
- Be fully believable in its capacity to deliver

A strong deductive argument is required to tailor the proposition for a client visit. The argument should be logic-based and should follow a line of reasoning triggered by the specific situation that client faces and focus on what is hindering the client from resolving the issue without you.

**Expanding and qualifying the warm client base**

When you have landed in the right Half Way House, there should be only one limiting factor regarding which clients or customers you can approach and connect with and that is you. You should be in a role that enables you to develop business, and by which I mean contacting clients using any and all communication channels. If previously you had an external facing role, then once you have settled into your new position you should send all your contacts a courtesy email or social media update regarding where you have arrived and your new remit. However, keep it light and social until you have orientated and cemented your proposition.

There are many contact strategies and customer relationship management applications available on the market. SalesForce.com is probably the most widely known. However, a simple Excel sheet can also provide for a systematic approach to contact management while you get started. Use Excel to manage a list of organisations, contacts, and actions and be disciplined in keeping it up to date. Contact management is pivotal to success. Making those 4 or 5 contacts every day and updating your contact log. A general rule of thumb I have lived by is "the more human and social the interaction, the greater the opportunity that is presented". Namely, email, text, cold calling, and social media may, at best, get you an introduction or open a door, but they will rarely lead to an opportunity. Opportunities come from meeting people, talking to them, and understanding them and their challenges. There is a diagnostic element to any professional services sale and this is most effectively done in person. The meeting builds trust and rapport and with this the most valuable information gets exchanged.

For me, engaging with the prospect client base is the most rewarding piece of providing a specialist service. What follows are a few basic recommendations on approach:

- Research your target company and client contact before making the appointment. You cannot afford to spend half a day travelling to and from a meeting that is not in the least bit qualified.
- Related to the above: Employ highly disciplined time management. Break the day up into chunks and if you have time allocated to business development, use it wisely.
- Ensure any introductory written messages (e.g. email or social media) are concise and precise in their meaning. People don't like reading waffly sales introductions.
- Always use the phone (not email) to follow up with prospect clients up until an appointment or need is established.
- In a prospect meeting, make every effort to connect on a social level before discussing business.
- Use open questions to gather information and don't overly

push for information.

- Always leave a prospect meeting with an agreed next action and date.

**Creation of thought leadership and soap box rights**

Before resigning from the corporation, you will have hopefully followed this guide by investing time in Principle 4 (above): Creating the Knowledge Base. As discussed in the previous chapter, this consists of a library of literary and digital assets all designed to keep you on the leading edge of your specialism.

To accentuate and to improve the value of your specialism, it will be important to create thought leadership. This is a skill that, just like any competence, will improve with practice. There is always a temptation to diverge from your specialism to follow tangential trending or hype related subjects. For example, in technology there is a lot of hype around the idea of "Big Data". For me, it is necessary to know about Big Data and its implications, but it's not core to my specialism so I don't put a lot of time into it. It is also a very crowded space and full of ambiguity just as its forbearer "business intelligence" was. Whereas, Machine to Machine (M2M) communications is key to my specialism and is an area that I need to study and write about.

Thought leadership may be described generically as "original educational content", and it can take many forms from articles to videos to brochures to presentations. When done correctly, it should help to bolster your value proposition and also provide a uniqueness of insight that will act as a "soapbox" to raise and amplify your voice in the market. Conceiving the original idea is often the hardest point in thought leadership, although it doesn't have to be *totally* original. The best pieces of thought leadership employ lateral thinking. As in the reference to Steve Jobs in the last section, thought leadership can combine two or more different ideas to generate a different approach to the your subject matter or specialism. For instance I have addressed the slow adoption of shared technology services in the Health Sector in particular the slow uptake of internet-based technologies due to proprietary and closed systems.

The key is to differentiate, to have a story with an angle; something that sets you apart and gives you the voice that you need to progress. I would recommend using the same deductive reasoning that you used to establish the value proposition. Namely, describe the situation, define the problem constraints, set out the key steps required to change the situation, and overcome the constraints.

Barbara Minto pioneered a similar approach - known as the Pyramid Approach - while working for top consulting firms in the 80's. The approach bound by the idea that all strong arguments are constructed like a pyramid. Led by a governing thought that addresses a problem, the argument is subsequently broken down into key lines or groups of like types of justification. This is a leading edge technique that is used to convey a persuasive argument by the most successful contemporary presenters and journalists. There is a lot written on the Pyramid Approach and its ability to create and indisputable argument so please Google it and learn as much as you can about deconstructing problems and structuring fully justified arguments for change or development.

Also, be careful to ensure that whatever content you are producing that it is   prepared correctly for the event, magazine, or meeting. Presentations should be visual NOT full of words, meeting slides should be brief and present workable insight, and magazine articles should inspire and provoke interest in the subject matter AND the author (i.e., you). So when writing thought leadership   do not forget to advertise yourself. There should be ample reference to your expertise and experience in the field. Stay focused on the overarching goal: to secure valuable and rewarding work and sustainable client relationships.

**Operate the sale**

Okay, this is where it gets neat (a word I am determined to revamp). You've escaped corporate, joined a small consultancy or a start up, warmed up your customer contact base over a several months, honed your value proposition, and released your first pieces of thought leadership into a few journals, your social network, and your company website. You are already feeling good about yourself, but there is still some residual doubt; it's completely natural. Your individual value and your proposition has not yet been road tested. But here comes the icing on the cake: A client responds to your proposition or thought leadership and requests that you complete a short assessment on a current programme they have in operation that lends itself to your area of specialism. Gotcha! This is a priceless moment. Your heart rate quickens. It's a small job but has good onward sales potential if you get it right. It may just be for an initial week or two week period, but it doesn't matter. This is the first sale from your own efforts and it's exciting. Because for the first time, possibly in your entire career, you are really leading and delivering on your own, *discrete, and individual unique value.* People are not working with you because the company has that job function - it is because they need your insight and specialism. When that client needs you, enjoy it. In actual fact, don't just enjoy it, bask in it for a while, just not for too long, as you now have to operate like there's no tomorrow. Your first clients *must* be reference clients - this is how the momentum starts.

Operating these first sales allows you to get the plane (value proposition) out of the hanger and off the runway. However, it needs to be completely flyable - you can not afford to crash through the perimeter fence or plough into low hills just off the runway. You need to get airborne and instill confidence in your client, so be completely prepared. If you are to perform a competency assessment, ensure that you are using analytics tools that are tried and tested. If you are structuring an outsourcing programme, make sure you have a tried and tested approach using templates, inventories, and software that can be employed quickly and systematically. Client meetings should be time boxed and follow a strict agenda, unless it's a social meeting or the client has other objectives. It doesn't matter if you are in to proofread, recruit talent, develop software, or advise on renewable energy - it makes no difference. You need to be prepared and come with a proven or demonstrable methodology. Do not just show up with a stream of consciousness or academic principles to test on your client. They are employing you for hard results, and most-likely to reduce some form of risk. This may seem obvious, but it is worth being emphatic in the initial client meetings. State your track record inside and outside of corporations, clarify your four step approach (or whatever it is), and explain why it delivers results.

These initial sales and operations will present the opportunity for you to review your shop front, your professional space - everything from social media, website, value proposition, and any events and forums that you have attended or plan to attend. Use the job, the approach, any feedback or sector knowledge that you acquire, to update and refine your marketing collateral. Real life operational problems and their actual resolution are so much more powerful than pure rhetoric and will serve to rapidly ground any unfounded grandiloquence. It is the anecdotes from these initial experiences that will exponentially enhance your unique value going forward.

**Escape Principle 6:** Develop and operate thought leadership. The best way to advance in business is through operating and reassessing the proposition.

# 8. All systems go

So, the former sections of this guide have presented you with an approach, which, should you want to, you can employ to exit stage left from a meaningless corporate void and venture out into the creation of independent professional value. A move to set yourself apart from the seething disgruntled mass commute silently frowning its way into and out of the concrete on a daily basis, and to pursue a more wholesome diet of life balanced with professional and personal experience. Sweet. So with this way forward in mind, this section looks at some of the tools and support systems that are available to help you in executing your Escape Plan.

## The Research

For exploring ideas in your field or related fields, there are some good free research tools available in the market. I would thoroughly recommend trying these before paying for a subscription to a specialist research or information service:

### iWhitepapers.com

This site is good for preliminary research. It covers technology, marketing and manufacturing, and provides access to a large database of white papers for the price of an email address.

Which, ultimately, I imagine will be used for marketing purposes. However, after a few years of using this service I am yet to receive a predatory mail. Also, I say preliminary research because the whitepapers are typically high-level and will give you a flavour of a subject area but no depth or insight.

### scholar.Google.com

From a free research standpoint, Google Scholar provides an incredible range of scholastic studies. However, a couple of major points here. Firstly, most of the research sites that you will access will provide abstract summaries only and will charge you for full access to the journal or article. Secondly, this information is by its nature highly academic and can be impracticable or inoperable, and as such is not directly business applicable. Nonetheless, it's always good to have a digest of the leading academic thinking at your finger tips. Note: When using this website, ensure you use the date filter in the left menu in order to surface contemporary thinking only.

### TechRepublic.com

This is a great research site for the technologically orientated, such as myself. The research covers most aspects of business related information technology, both from a vertical industry and horizontal business processes standpoint. Naturally, if you are breaking out of corporate to become a maritime archeologist this site is likely to provide limited insight.

### TradePub.com

In the event that you are a maritime archeologist or exploring a less than mainstream specialism, I would recommend

TradePub.com. Just about every trade journal in existence can be found at this site with little hidden gems such as the Innovative Egg Industry and Pig International.

### The Website

Okay, so to keep it snappy, this is a cut to the chase recommendation on website creation. If you are like me, you will want to influence design and provide all the content for your website. One of my sites is www.iomie.com. I designed the schema with simple online design tools and wrote and uploaded the content. Alternatives are available on the market ranging from the wholly bespoke approach of employing a web design studio through to finding a web host provider that exhibits an array of static templates to choose from.

Getting a web developer to code your website from scratch is okay as long as you want to pay ongoing administration and change fees for the upkeep and maintenance of the site. Alternatively, buying a static web template will exude a low cost site and may significantly under-represent your value proposition. A good product with a poor website misses its market potential and will serve to put potential clients off. It needs to look the business and create the right first impression.

So, ideally, to have your cake and eat it you will need a website builder that is user friendly and allows full customisation without relying on programming. There are a few leading providers on the market and many new entrants. Below is a checklist for must-have features:

1. The website provider operates HTML5 (this is the leading HTML website technology at the time of writing). This provides for greater flexibility and animation without the use of Flash or other such fast fading technology plug-ins.

2. Ensure the provider service includes the domain name, email services, and a wide variety of starting frames or templates as part of the package.

3. Ensure that there is a drag and drop facility that is easy and responsive to use so that content and media can easily be imported, tagged, and edited.

4. Ensure that the templates do not use static frames and look antiquated. They should use the full screen and be flexible as to where content is placed and formatted.

5. There should be a big bag of widgets and full social media integration.

6. The website builder tool should be quick and responsive, allowing previews and publishing in real-time.

These selection criteria considerably narrow a wide field of providers. I have    identified three reputable high performance providers operating in this space. The first is www.wix.com arguably in the lead regarding its user base with over 20 million users, or so it claims. The further two are www.web.com (a priceless domain name) and www.weebly.com. I am close to discounting web.com, as their product has not yet been developed to make it fully mobile compatible. Which, given that these days 65% of web access is through a mobile device, is a bit daft. Weebly.com provides unlimited storage, unlike

WIX.com, which is a plus if you require an e-commerce or digital assets web site, however Weebly are shy on email integration. WIX will provide email accounts for a small additional fee. So these guys are the leaders of the pack and, as far as I can see, are constantly developing their product to make it more intuitive, adaptable, and inter-operable. There are literally 100's of others, although these three are a safe bet for the immediate future.

**The Social Media**

Social Media is a multi-headed hydra of a tool. As previously mentioned, like a Swiss army knife, if you choose the wrong blade its impact can be potentially damaging. If you don't get the right message to the right market at the right time, the response will be disappointing or at best unexpected.

So, why is social media so irregular? Well, essentially it boils down to values and markets. Most individuals join a social media tool (let's use the example of LinkedIn) to socially communicate with other professionals, look for jobs, or read content. Most people do not join to be sold to. Moving a person's behaviour from social values to market values is a tricky shift for any form of communication. We generally mistrust people who try to appear to be socialising while their real intention is to trade. However, as Facebook has recently discovered, the blurred line here is the one of creating awareness. You can still advertise, create awareness, and show insight so that when people do recognise a need (latent or otherwise) they can come to you. You will note that sites like Etsy and Pintrest are crossing this divide, however it is still really a browsers market based on advertisement rather than active selling through direct communication.

Targeted selling on a social media site should not be at the cost of a relevant relationship. Namely, the sales message and targeted need should either be accurately identified or alternatively the potential risk of degradation of the relationship considered immaterial. However, this principally applies to cold prospecting. When using your personal contacts, the degree of sales strength of the message can depend on the nature of the relationship and whether you are communicating 1 on 1, 1 to many, or using them as a referral, an interim meeting, or an end point of sale. My personal preference is to use social networks to create awareness and to generate meetings or calls for further discovery and diagnostic work. I have not once tried to create a sale directly online. It doesn't work for a consultative service where the problem discovery requires quite an extensive initial face to face conversation.

Set Up

I will illustrate the use of a social network using LinkedIn, a social media network designed specifically for professionals. You will first need to join LinkedIn and set up your profile if you have not done so already. I recommend a minimalist approach to your profile - the scarcest resource of any professional is time and, although you might like to write like Dostojevski and philosophise like Neitzsche, it is unlikely that it will be read. As covered in "Setting Up The Shop Front", the value proposition, brand, and experience needs to be consistent across all public facing messaging, so copy and paste from your website where necessary. As part of a summary introduction, bullet your areas of specialism and complete your profile.

Note that on your page, you can add Project and Work Experience. As your projects develop and increase project experience, it will become more relevant as a working track record. When adding either work or project to your profile, cite the job type, and scope; then, most importantly, what was to be achieved (quantitively, if at all possible) and how you achieved it. Again, keep this succinct and always keep the jobs most relevant to your core specialism and proposition at the top of the list.

Okay, so once you have established a concise and impacting private page (and added a professional mug shot) you can continue by setting up a company page and/or establish professional groups. On a small note: It's always a worthwhile investment to have a professional photo taken. It's all part of your brand, no matter how trivial you think it may be. It demonstrates attention to detail and an appropriate perception of your own professionalism. After all, if you can't take yourself seriously nobody else will. Humour can come with familiarity, for prospecting and presentation purposes you need to be the real deal. Focused, on point, and results-orientated.

Company Page

A Company Page is a relatively recent addition to LinkedIn and supports the company having a profile on LinkedIn in addition to the individual.

**Tip:** Be warned that company pages can be linked back to their owner's professional page so do not launch a company page if you are trying to operate below the radar of a corporation. You will soon be discovered.

I would recommend that whether you are operating as a sole trader, with associates or as a limited a company that you set up a company page for the 4 following reasons:

1. It extends the shop front
2. It can be used to improve brand and proposition identity
3. It can be used to make targeted announcements
4. It can be used for hiring and soliciting business

Once you have the dimensioning of your company logo/picture correct and uploaded (which is a tad tedious and needs to be addressed by LinedIn), you should offer a small overview using the key words that you would expect to be used in a search for your services. By way of example, the description of my job site reads: "Leading and facilitating technology transformation projects for the health sector with cost effective consultancy and resourcing". Like many, you may want to use your Company Page as your company blog. There is also now a facility to add "ShowCase" pages to enable you to draw attention to one particular aspect of your organisation or service (e.g. free project assessments or white papers).

Groups
The Professional Profile page allows you to manage your profile and direct connections. The company page edifies the company image, updates, and communicates with contacts while the Group options give you the wider network exposure that you will need to branch out.

LinkedIn Groups exist to amplify the networked voice, to stimulate new connections and engagement between people with similar needs or interests. Your Company Page can host a group and can feature up to three groups, but the group will still need to be set up by your profile.

Guidance on setting up a group:

The set up of a group can serve an element of your value proposition, all of your value proposition, or at a minimum foster a dialogue that engenders positive thoughts and considerations about your services. However, there are thousands of groups and, these days professionals are picky about which ones they belong to. After all, who you affiliate with is a significant part of your brand. There is a tried and tested South American saying: "Me muestras con quein andas y te digo quien eres" or "Show me who you walk with and I'll tell you who you are". The simple sayings are always the best. When setting up a group, remember to:

1. Be specific about the niche or subject category in the group name and description.
2. Make sure it is an "open group" with member pre-approval.
3. Closely manage and monitor group for spam and value destructive messaging
4. Promote your group to your existing contacts - a maximum of 50 per day is tolerated by the application.

How to grow a group:

Aside from regularly inviting your contacts - which is by far the best way to get an initial attendance - you can

also cheat by artificially growing your group by paying someone to add members. **Tip:** This is a short cut and just like most short cuts it is susceptible to backfire. You will receive irrelevant posts and need to spend time pruning and managing content that you clearly didn't want associated in your group communications.

The advantage of establishing a group is the access to a predefined target market. For your audience to remain YOUR target market, you really need to grow it organically. Messaging and contributing responsibly to other groups set up on related subject matter is the best way to get exposure on your thought leadership outside of your immediate contact base. You can always copy a link to your website and group page into your posts. However, be careful that if the group manager sees you as a direct competitor and/or a poacher of members you may find yourself quickly losing your membership.

Look for group members that are asking questions that align to the type of services you have to offer. This is an incredible marketing tool if used correctly. You can identify and communicate rapidly with a contact base that you already know shares a similar interest.

However, a **MAJOR** word of warning here that cannot be reiterated enough is: **NO HARD SELLING**. Hard selling is not "social" and you will rapidly find yourself alienated. Do not abuse your network. Treat them as you would like to be treated.

**Other Small Business Support Tools**

We have covered a good amount of ground so far and highlighted tasks and services that will help your business spread its wings. What we have also demonstrated is that there is a fair bit to do even before you start billing your hours. Time and creativity are your most valuable resources, so below are some cheap (and free) office automation tools that you can use to "box clever" and release more time for creativity.

1.  Free Office Applications:
Google Docs and Open Office are amongst a number of free office software services. Google Docs is a "Cloud Service" – namely, it is accessible through the internet, whereas Open Office is a downloadable freeware so you can work where you want when you want. With both, you have Word, Presentation, and Excel type capabilities. Microsoft 365 gives you the option to work online and off-line with the standard Microsoft office applications – however, this comes at a small monthly charge.

2.  Contact Management:
Depending on the nature and scale of your business, you may not need customer relationship management software. However, when you start getting multiple concurrent leads and opportunities you will need to manage your contact base. There are various types of Contact Management services available. For example, off the shelf software and cloud services. I would recommend SalesForce.com Contact Management at $5 per

month to get started. You can try it for free with no strings attached. If you require a high level of customisation then I would recommend SugarCRM which is fully customisable in either a cloud or download format.


3.    Additional Support Staff:

If there is one incredibly useful resource to have throughout your escape, it has to be and extra pair of hands. Also, while you're operating a job you may need additional support for administrative tasks or research activities that do not necessarily add immediate value to your services. The three companies I recommend are www.elance.com, www.odesk.com, and www.freelancer.com. You can find just about any type of business support and at any price on these sites, such as: proofreading, website building, online marketing, report/technical writing, market research, translation, and general business administration. In my experience, oDesk is best set up for hourly paid work while all three are good for fixed price jobs. You only pay when you are satisfied with the work and if the worker claims hours for work that you are not happy with you reserve the right to dispute and not pay.


**Tip:** 1) Be ULTRA clear with your work objectives and acceptance criteria    and 2) You get what you pay for. If your project is complex, critical, or time dependent, it is worth paying a little more to secure quality.


4.    Project Management:

Depending on the complexity of your business and client base, you may benefit from the use of project and/or programme management software. For a simple task based system that is free to use, I would recommend www.FreedCamp.com. It is a basic way to track project milestones, allocate tasks, and collaborate on project progress. For a more complex project management, a service such as www.thrivesolo.com is a good platform for managing costs, resource, and billing. Naturally, with this type of service there comes a charge starting at around £10 per month per user. However, if you need this service I would venture that your project revenues will more than justify the expense.

These tools and support services will give you a taste of what is available to help you at little or no cost. This list is far from exhaustive and is at best illustrative. Before choosing any one service, I would spend a small amount of your valuable time in getting a list of the top rated services in each category and making an informed decision for yourself. My recommendations above are just mainstream safe bets as I would need a further hundred pages to describe all the small office  automation tools available on the market. Perhaps the topic of a different book.


**Design Principle 7:** Use social media to amplify your voice to new target markets, generate leads, share experience and create dialogue with prospects.

**Design Principle 8:** No hard selling using Social Media. Hard selling is not sociable! If there is a sales interest take it **off-line** for further discussion.

**Design Principle 9:** Box clever by using business automation tools and low cost support resource for any work that does not drive sufficient or immediate value for your business.

# 9. The escape plan

At risk of stating the very obvious, the benefit of having a plan of action is that it allows you to execute in stages, clarify the parts of the whole, and to deliver in a time frame that works for you using the resources and time that you have at your disposal. The best plans are steered by timelines that should be on the cusp of attainable and driven by a compelling event that focuses the outcome. The worst plans have little or no consequence of inactivity, have no clear milestones, and non-specific results or objectives.

As discussed in the Prologue to this book, all the major step changes I have made as a professional I have achieved through tactical planning and all of the sometimes long periods of "dormancy" or active inertia have equally been accompanied by the lack of planning. For this reason, I have come to the rather obvious conclusion that to create change in one's own trajectory you must plan for it. The best delivery plans are defined by the following characteristics:

- Keep the plan on the cusp of an implementable time frame: Keep it tight. Too much slack in the process will just create distraction.
- Set realistic and measurable milestones: When following the steps outlined in this guide, ensure each milestone has a qual-

ity assurance checklist so you know when the criteria for delivery have been satisfied.

- Work into a compelling event: This could be a birthday, a work anniversary, a holiday, or a more business orientated goal such as number of leads, clients, or contracts.
- Be disciplined about change control: Don't just let the plan slide. If you need to re-peg it due to an unforeseen event, set aside 30 minutes to do so.
- And lastly, print the plan off and blue tack it to the inside of your wardrobe door or office wall so you can see it every day. Rarely does a good plan put in a draw deliver.

**Timelines and Milestones**

Below are a few suggestions regarding the milestones set out in this book. What is important to note is that these are best estimates that are based on the experiences of various individuals who have gone through this process successfully.

**Self assessment:**

This stage should be thoroughly considered. Active Inertia is an often deceptive and allusive state to diagnose and has many attributes to account for. Companies are designed to create the illusion of progress and employees have a natural tendency to hedge against change. This accompanied by our well developed skills in self persuasion leads to a mind state that can be tricky to diagnose. Depending on circumstance, I would recommend that at least one or two months is taken to assess your state of inertia. Document what motivates you about your role on a weekly basis, and where the issues and opportunities lie. Look at the probability of corporate succession and talk to others that have made internal changes. Also, look at the long game. My own definition of hell is to take a last breath knowing I did not do what I could have done. I pursue no regrets as a life goal!

**Establish unique value:**

This stage is essential in developing a knowledge base but also the evidence base for escape. However, don't let this stage drag. So time it out. List what you need to accomplish in this step and stick to it. List the courses you need to attend, the events you need to go to, the types of information you want in your knowledge base, and any additional competencies that you need to acquire. Then draw a line under the list. Do not let it manifest into a shopping list of the unattainable as a pretext for no action. Ideally, it should take you no longer than a few months to build up any residual competencies and a solid information repository.

**Setting up the shop front:**

Setting up the shop front can be an iterative process completed conjointly with step 2 (above). However, ONLY if it is below the radar when you are still gamefully employed. Establishing the value proposition, creating, and fine-tuning marketing and messaging should all be thorough behind the scenes work. Avoid the pitfall of marketing a brand and proposition only to change and iterate it as your depth of knowledge on the subject area deepens. Specialism and value come from consistency and acuity of insight, not flighty changes in interest and direction. I would recommend spending 1 - 2 months setting up the shop front. However, only generate awareness of your undertaking when it is polished, shiny, and stable.

## The Half Way House:

The time dedicated to the "sandpit" or test ground for your brand and proposition is specific to the nature, criticality, and complexity of the proposition itself.  If your desire is to fly solo as a picture framing company vs. the outsourcing of surgical medical systems, you may want to spend more or less time in the Half Way House developing the warm customer base and getting rich on the job experience. In reality this phase can last anywhere from 1 month to over a year. What is essential is that you are meeting the Half Way House criteria of operating on your own proposition collateral and thought leadership and thereby generating future business opportunities and professional unique value.

## All systems go:

The final checkpoint. Self diagnosis complete, unique professional value established and validated, shop front constructed, and Half Way House proposition test runs and client acceptance complete. All systems go is a final step in ensuring that you have all the business support systems in place to allow you to run like the wind and deliver quality to your first customers and clients. Spend a week running the checks, ensuring consistency then push the plane out the hanger.

Below is an illustration of the 5 Month Escape Plan. Naturally, this depends heavily on the degree of overlap between stages and the length of time spent on stage 4. The Half Way House normally has a natural expiry as clients express their interests to work directly with you and avoid the supplemental fees associated with the overheads of your chosen interim organisation.

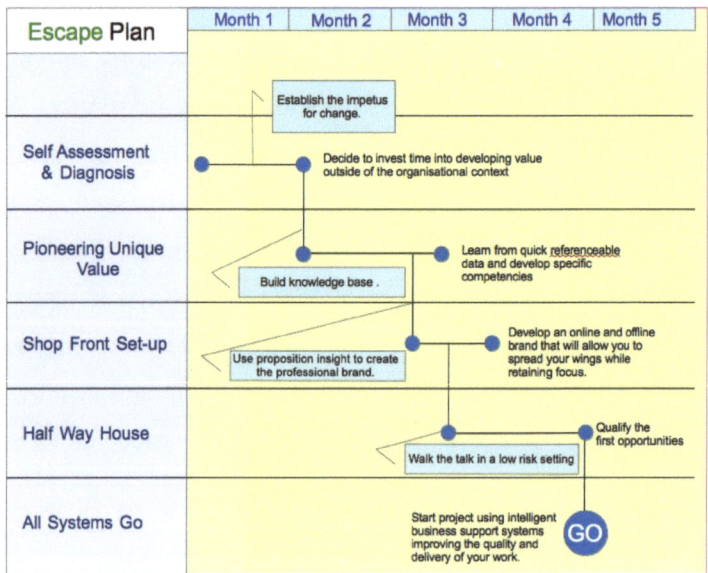

## On a final note:

I would like to point out that I have invariably found that the Escape Plan will elevate the professional within the corporate environment almost as a bi-product of the individual's intent. The increased value, confidence, independence, and professional orientation of the employee is more times than not picked up by management who, as a natural response, will try to harness the competence by improving the role. The outcome for the employee in large companies is normally limited over time by management churn or changing priorities, so for those that undergo this experience I recommend that you keep your eye firmly on the end goal, namely, the Escape. Best wishes, et bon voyage!

\

# Appendix: Escape principles

### Escape Principle 1.

Do not wait around for the pay off unless it is imminent and certain. Your time is of greater value. You are voluntarily bound to your organisation and you can leave when you want. If the time is right, move now, otherwise your dissonance with the company may well cost you your self esteem and ambition before it costs the company a cent. Naturally, if redundancy is imminent and certain, don't be a chump either.

### Escape Principle 2.

Diagnosis of Active Inertia is a good thing and means that remedy can begin. Recognising your lack of appetite for the corporate belief system is a major step forward. Do not become a resident cynic. If your goals and the company's game plan for you no longer align, then change the game field. Don't persist in kicking a football at a set of cricket stumps.

### Escape Principle 3.

Connect to a unique and genuine interest. Find something to get lost in. A specialism that you want to read up on; That you want to write about.; That you want to help people with. Where it takes discipline to stop doing it rather than to get started.

### Escape Principle 4.

Build the knowledge centre. Extend your insight and value with easily accessible information. Become the thought leader and/or take the specialism in a different direction. Increasingly, disciplines are becoming blurred, the subject boundaries indoctrinated by countless educational systems are eroding and giving way to creativity and hybrid approaches to problem solving. *Behavioural Economics* is a good example.

### Escape Principle 5.

Get the messaging of your services value proposition(s) honed and polished before it is exposed to your public. Don't roll out anything less than high quality. This is your retirement and your kid's future on the line. Make it superior and charge a premium for it. Look the part, sound the part, and deliver the goods. Make people happy.

### Escape Principle 6.

Develop and operate thought leadership. The best way to advance in business is through operating and reassessing. Nothing happens in a PowerPoint deck. It is only through application and operational assessment that we refine our business practices and improve. So be active, get involved, and implement your approach.

### Escape Principles 7 and 8.

Social Media - amplify your voice to new target markets, generate leads, share experience, and create dialogue with prospects. However, do not hard sell using Social Media. Use Social Media as a show room to demonstrate and create awareness of your capabilities. If someone likes the look of the product, they will enquire further.

## Escape Principle 9.

Lastly, box clever. Use business automation tools and low cost support resource for work that does not create value for your client. The internet was designed for the independent professional: it democratises information and provides an ever increasing amounts of tools and resources. These assets allow you to focus your efforts and deliver quality and expert guidance to the client.